I LOVE
HERMIT CRABS

by Harold T. Rober

BUMBA BOOKS™

LERNER PUBLICATIONS ◆ MINNEAPOLIS

Note to Educators:

Throughout this book, you'll find critical thinking questions. These can be used to engage young readers in thinking critically about the topic and in using the text and photos to do so.

Lerner Publications Company
A division of Lerner Publishing Group, Inc.
241 First Avenue North
Minneapolis, MN 55401 USA

For reading levels and more information, look up this title at www.lernerbooks.com.

Library of Congress Cataloging-in-Publication Data

Names: Rober, Harold T., author.
Title: I love hermit crabs / by Harold T. Rober.
Description: Minneapolis : Lerner Publications, [2016] | Series: Bumba books—Pets are the best | Audience: Ages 4–8. | Audience: K to grade 3. | Includes bibliographical references and index.
Identifiers: LCCN 2016003157 (print) | LCCN 2016017081 (ebook) | ISBN 9781512414189 (lb : alk. paper) | ISBN 9781512415278 (pb : alk. paper) | ISBN 9781512415285 (eb pdf)
Subjects: LCSH: Hermit crabs as pets—Juvenile literature.
Classification: LCC SF459.H47 R63 2016 (print) | LCC SF459.H47 (ebook) | DDC 639.67—dc23

LC record available at https://lccn.loc.gov/2016003157

Manufactured in the United States of America
1 – VP – 7/15/16

Expand learning beyond the printed book. Download free, complementary educational resources for this book from our website, www.lerneresource.com.

Table of Contents

Pet Hermit Crabs

Hermit crabs are fun pets.

They like to be near other crabs.

We have two of them.

Hermit crabs need a large tank.

Hermit crabs like to climb.

We put toys inside.

We cover the bottom
of the tank with sand.

It is deep.

The crabs bury
themselves.

**Why do
you think
hermit crabs
bury themselves?**

Hermit crabs like to hide.

They hide in their shells.

They hide inside the tank too.

What else
do you think
hard shells are
useful for?

11

We put a heater and a wet

sponge in the tank.

We clean the tank each month.

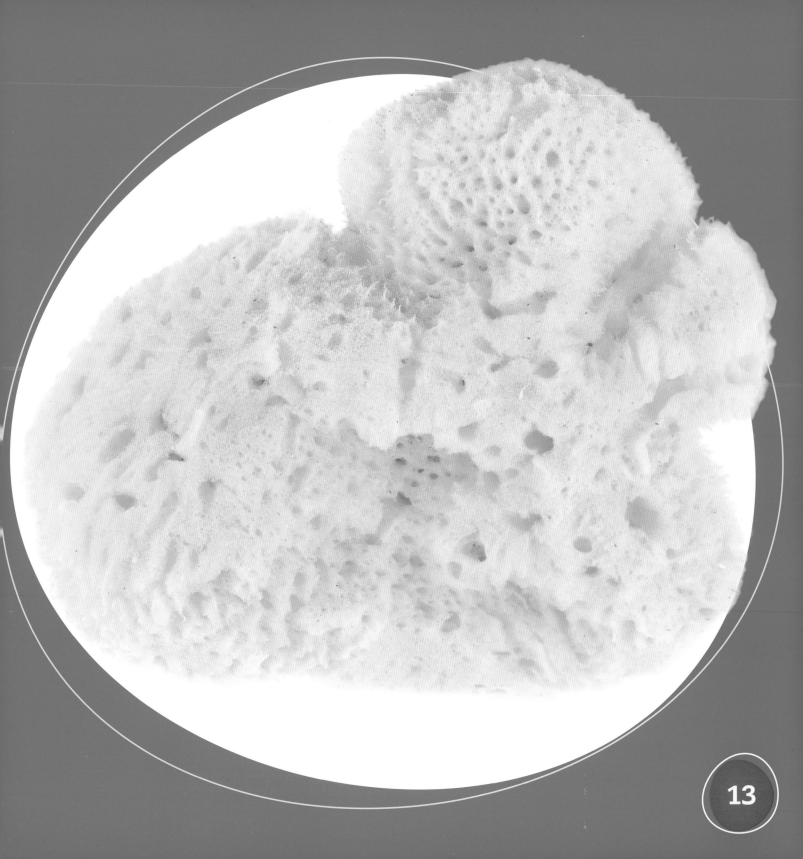

13

Hermit crabs grow.

We put bigger shells in the tank.

The crabs change shells when they are ready.

Why do you think hermit crabs need bigger shells?

Hermit crabs need water.

They need food too.

We buy the food at a pet store.

We hold our crabs.

We put our hands

out flat.

The crabs stand

on our hands.

Hermit crabs can live for ten years.

They make great pets!

Hermit Crab Supplies

tank

sponge

sand

shells

Picture Glossary

bury

to hide under something

sand

small, loose pieces of rock and shell

shells

hard outer coverings or cases

sponge

a pad that absorbs water

23

Index

Read More

Armentrout, David. *Help! I Have a Hermit Crab.* Vero Beach, FL: Rourke Publishing, 2011.

Carr, Aaron. *Hermit Crab.* New York: AV2 by Weigl, 2016.

Silverstein, Alvin. *Hermit Crabs: Cool Pets!* Berkeley Heights, NJ: Enslow Elementary, 2011.

Photo Credits

FRONT ROW CENTER 3

FRONT ROW CENTER 3

ERIK HILDEBRANDT

Steve Oliver demonstrating his night show wing-tip fountains at twilight for the sake of the camera high above the Terre Haute Air Fair in Indiana. If you have never been, put Terre Haute on your "must see" list as it is the biggest little show there is and by far the best organized.

DEDICATION

This book was created during a time of significant change and adjustment for my family and me. It stands as testament to the dedication and strength of our extended family and all our friends around the country that such an original creative project with the depth of this book can be conceived of and captured in the short span of a single airshow season. Without their unconditional love and support, Christine and I could never have been able to carry on, let alone flourish again if it were not for all the selfless sacrifices made on our behalf. For all those contributions and supporters out there, this book is dedicated to you.

Thank you all very much.

Erik Hildebrandt

FRONT ROW CENTER 3

Published in the United States of America by:
Cleared Hot Media, Inc.
Stillwater, Minnesota
erik@vulturesrow.com
651-430-3344

First Imprint
ISBN 0-9674040-6-1
Printed in CHINA

John Klatt pulls in behind the MNANG C-130 based in Minneapolis for a photo flight over Lake Superior with Duluth-based MNANG F-16C piloted by LTCOL Patrick Freeman. Our boys: Roan the Brave and his Brother's Keeper, Finn.

ACKNOWLEDGEMENTS

Besides all the usual suspects that make FRONT ROW CENTER possible, a few folks stepped forward and helped in ways that made my life not only easier, but safer too. Jim Obwa, Dale Snodgrass, Col. Mark Sheehan, Jeff Hall, Doug Rozendaal and Bob Murphy all manned the controls of the crusty yet charmingly original O-2A I now own and use as an aerial station wagon getting me and my gear to and from shows. It also pulls duty as an outstanding and super smooth platform to shoot from. These guys know their stuff and each helped me build the experience to know what could or could not be done safely in this plane.

David Nilson lent me tremendous support by writing several of the essays that follow. He saved my bacon on my recent F-14 Tomcat book by catching and correcting all of the typos and continuity issues that riddled the text of the first edition volume. Dave Nilsen is a lifelong naval and military historian, a gift that he credits to his late grandfather, Edwin D. "Easy Dog" Robinson, who was a Machinists Mate aboard Pacific Fleet S-Boats in the 1920s. Dave also collects Navy patches, T-shirts, postcards, and cruise videos. Dave drives a Blue Angel blue-and-gold pick up truck that he has customized to transport his three American Eskimo dogs, USS Saratoga, USS Constellation, and USS Coral Sea. His favorite airshow is NAS Oceana.

The Blues have long been my most challenging and willing photo subjects game for most anything I could dream up. This year I owe my most sincere gratitude to Boss Foley and "Ghost" Kasper for allowing me to the chance to once again push the envelope by chasing the Delta with former BA solo Loni Anderson to capture the entire formation as a detached floater. This rare exception to the Blues rule of never flying formation with non-demo aircraft allowed us to capture some truly unique images. Thanks and congratulations for Sixty Years of NAVAIR Demo perfection.

The following airshow organizers graciously hosted me and made it possible to capture these performers in their element:
Dennis Dunbar – Terre Haute Air Fair, Ryan Kern– Monaco Air/Duluth Airshow, Ken Hopper– Quad Cities Airshow
And special thanks to Larry Gallogly, Mark Sheehan and Arthur Floru and the rest of my RI Family – Quonset Point, RI RIANG,

-Erik Hildebrandt

Patty Wagstaff orbiting upsidedown over Lake Superior during a visit to the home base of Cirrus Design in Duluth, Minnesota. Photo plane was the O-2A Skymaster with Doug Rozendaal at the controls.

PREFACE

The FRONT ROW CENTER brand of airshow images and books have become the industry showcase standard for pilots and performers from every spectrum of the circuit. As quickly as the landscape evolves and changes, there seems to be a fresh edition of FRC to capture and present those new and often improved acts in photographs that preserve forever the feeling of pride and accomplishment that these players have for their performances. The pilots that I have flown with over the past 8 years have continuously caused me to grow and expand my own skills to keep pace with the innovations that they make in the skies. Finding new and dramatic ways to capture their unique approaches to aviation has become more and more difficult, but more than any previous edition of FRC, this volume represents the greatest leap forward in my abilities as an air-to-air photographer. This season, I piloted my own plane from show to show and often utilized it as the principal photo-platform, obviously enlisting the help highly qualified and skilled pilots to lead the actual formations. This infusion of first-hand experience as pilot-in-command certainly contributed to these breakthroughs and afforded me new perspectives on how to safely arrange these amazing pilots and their incredibly high performing aircraft in ways never before attempted. "Never before attempted" has become a theme throughout the FRONT ROW CENTER series, and it is what makes these images so compelling to look at to try and figure out just how the heck they are created. From time to time I have had to correct false assumptions that these images are computer fabrications. They are not. To that end, I have begun referencing any digital manipulations in the caption details for each photo. Regardless of the technical specifics behind the making of these pictures, I invite you to enjoy this book and it's performers. We had every bit as much fun as it seems, and you can bet there will be future editions of FRC that again will break new ground and push the envelope of aviation photography.

Thank you all for empowering my passion for flight!

−Erik Hildebrandt

Matt Chapman leads Michael Mancuso over the Gulf of Mexico off the coast of St. Petersburg, Florida. Photo ship was the O-2A Skymaster piloted by Bob Murphy.

STEVE OLIVER &
SUZANNE ASBURY-OLIVER

In an industry full of talented and well-known aviators, Steve Oliver and Suzanne Asbury-Oliver learned long ago that one plus one is greater than two. They have perfected the concept of "divide and conquer" by providing the airshow world with both power and grace and they do it with such a love for flying that any first-time observer is quickly baptized a life-long fan.

Clockwise from top left. Jude Dennis confers with Steve Oliver just prior to his Oshkosh performance. Steve Oliver strapping into the highly modified de Haviland Chipmunk with all of his Oregon Aero upgrades that help make it the most comfortable Chipmunk around. Opposite page: Going over the top of the photo ship Skymaster. Steve Oliver prepares to fire off the wing-tip fountain of sparks over the Terre Haute Air Fair.

For each, their love affair with flying began as kids. While Suzanne was growing up in Oregon, she was first exposed to the world of soaring at age fourteen, when she accompanied her dad to the local glider base where her mother had arranged a birthday flight for him. His enthusiasm for flying gliders towed Suzanne aloft and the two of them immediately began soaring instruction and ultimately purchased a Switzer 1-26 sailplane. Throughout high school, Suzanne steadily advanced. She earned her sailplane private ratings while in high school and her power ratings the year after graduation.

In Steve's case, his father was also the catalyst who sparked the aviation passion that burns so brightly within. His earliest childhood memory is of attending the Quincy, Illinois airshow and specifically being drawn to the military jets on display. His dad was a local farmer in nearby Missouri. After securing a coveted daytime mail-carrying route that insured a steady supplemental income, he purchased a Piper Vagabond and carved out a tiny strip on the farm from which to operate the tail dragger. Steve took his first flight at age twelve and began formal instruction after high school, at age eighteen. Within eleven months of his first lesson, he had his commercial and CFI ratings and was flying airshows, towing banners and flight instructing for his instructor. At the same time he was taking flight lessons, Steve was learning aeromechanics at the Kansas City, Missouri downtown airport plus working full time for an FBO at Fairfax airport in Kansas City, Kansas. Shortly thereafter, he took over the operation of a "flight school" that he operated from a farmer's field in Bethany, Missouri. Before long, as the Vietnam conflict was building, Steve voluntarily enlisted in the Army, and served his country as an air traffic controller. Upon his return, he spent the 60's and 70's giving flight instruction; offering charter flights and crop dusting; flying mail and cargo; and corporate flying.

By the time Steve and Suzanne met in 1981, both were full-time pilots. Steve was towing advertising banners around the country.

Steve and Suzanne fly together in the late afternoon sunlight near Oshkosh. Opposite page: Steve and Suzanne start and end each of their flights with a kiss. Suzanne and wonder-dog PAX after a long day of skywriting at the Terre Haute Air Fair. PAX was named after the PAX River or Patuxent River Naval Air Station by famed Navy F-14 Tomcat pilot Dale Snodgrass.

Suzanne had been a flight instructor and charter pilot for nearly three years before joining Pepsi Cola's rejuvenated skywriting operation in 1980. By 1981, she had taken over operation of the program. Pepsi pioneered the first commercial skywriting campaign in 1931, employing fourteen pilots around the country to spell out "PEPSI COLA" in the skies over county fairs, major cities and crowded beaches from coast to coast. For Suzanne, this freestyle art form of flying combined the freedom, challenges and skills that first drew her to soaring while providing a regular means to restore the nearly lost art of skywriting in an open-cockpit biplane for spectators across the country.

Fate smiled on these two wing nuts on the first weekend in May 1981, over the grounds of the Kentucky Derby. Both were operating their aircraft in support of the races and were introduced between flights. Eleven months later, they were married. And so began the longest run in aviation history of a sponsored husband- and- wife airshow team. For twenty-seven consecutive seasons, Suzanne flew skywriting missions for Pepsi while Steve supported and grew the program to include the first-ever aerobatic routine for the soft drink maker.

While it is the airborne side of their lives together that the public is most familiar with, friends who know Suzanne and Steve are equally amazed by their accomplishments as professional road warriors. Their twenty-seven year run with Pepsi kept them on the road thirty-three weeks of every fifty-two week season, starting the very first day they met. But instead of succumbing to the debilitating effects of chronic homesickness, they simply made their home the road, literally. More than any two people I have met, Suzanne and Steve have constructed a system of balance, comfort and contentment into the endlessly fluid world on the professional airshow circuit that normally burns most performers out by the end of each season. In fact, we should all be so fortunate as to enjoy just one facet of the multiple alternative lifestyles that Suzanne and Steve have engineered for themselves to combat the effects of airshow seasonal exhaustion syndrome.

It would seem to most of us that the concept of "home" is rooted in stability and routine. With Suzanne and Steve, their stability is based on flexibility, and the routine is comprised of variety. First and foremost, the primary residence, based solely on the amount of time spent there, is the premium Monaco motor coach in which they caravan from site to site like the modern day gypsies they become during the season.

When they have time enough between shows to justify airline seats, they either head for their mountain retreat in Steamboat Springs, Colorado, or the wind blows them down to the sea where they stow away on their 55-foot motor-yacht that awaits them in the Bahamas. There they put down anchor at one of hundreds of tropical islands, soaking in the quiet tranquility that soothes their souls after weeks of performing amidst the roar and crowds of the airshow circuit. The decision as to where they should rest up between shows seems to lie with the weather and on the whim of the tides. Either way, as in the rest of their lives, Suzanne and Steve get recharged together in the epitome of style.

Obviously, the system of their success on the road hinges on creature comfort. It is no coincidence that Steve was the first airshow pilot to be product-supported by Oregon Aero. It was 1989, the year Steve introduced his newly refurbished 1956 de Havilland Chipmunk –SkyDancer– to the airshow circuit. Mike Dennis founded Oregon Aero with his wife, Jude, that same year.

Mike is always innovating product solutions to improve comfort and performance in communities where environmental pressures create fatigue and oftentimes pain. The incredible spinning and twisting, coupled with the incredible g-forces exerted during Steve's SkyDancer performances, presented Mike with an ideal laboratory in which to test and develop the seat padding and helmet technologies that have become the company's hallmarks.

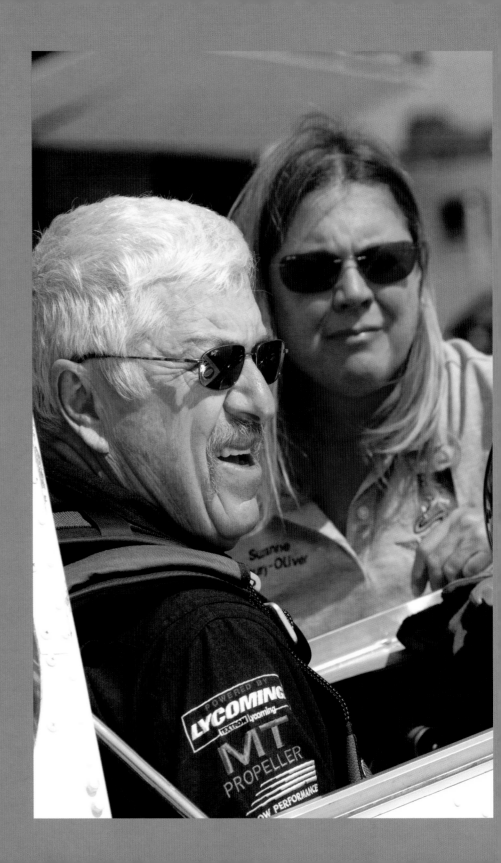

Suzanne is a master skywriter with both the talent of an artist and the skills of a test pilot. It is a lot harder than it looks to make it look as good as she does.

18 FRC3 Steamboat Springs resident photographer Don Tudor made this incredible time-lapse image of Steve Oliver flying his famous night pyro performance over downtown Steamboat Springs, Colorado where he and Suzanne retreat in their off hours. Don braved sub-zero temps and risked his camera freezing to bring us this image. Thanks, Don.

Rockin' and rollin' with the smoke pouring out, Steve Oliver wows the crowd at the Terre Haute Air Fair.

Today, the technologies that were first tried and tested with Steve and Suzanne in the airshow world have made tremendous improvements to the quality of life and service for professionals well beyond aviation. Mike and Jude are most proud of their accomplishments with US and foreign military units serving in Iraq and Afghanistan, where Oregon Aero's aviation and ballistic helmet padding systems have been adopted by thousands of ground forces, military pilots and armored vehicle crews. Oregon Aero helmet upgrade kits provide superior comfort, protection, stability, waterproofing and buoyancy for troops who need to live in their helmets.

Perhaps the best illustration of Mike's talent and insight into improving tactical flight environments is the introduction of the first-ever ejection seat cushion found in the F-22 Raptor. Up until this latest incarnation of the lifesaving ejection system, pilots sat on a flat, unpadded seat bottom because the incredible acceleration forces that occur at the initial phases of an ejection had to be transferred directly onto the pilot to avoid dissimilar acceleration that would likely break their backs. Ask any fighter pilot what limits their mission endurance more than anything else and they will tell you it is the butt-numbing effects of the unpadded ejection seat. Not any more.

In 2005, when Pepsi decided to retire its skywriting and airshow marketing program, Mike and Jude Dennis saw the incredible opportunity to showcase Oregon Aero's diverse and cutting-edge product line by partnering with their longtime friends and guinea pigs, Steve and Suzanne. Today, instead of seeing Pepsi among the clouds over Oshkosh, you'll be looking up at Suzanne's trademark smiley face winking down and grinning about her life on the road with a man and a dog and the three simple words: "Painless, Safer, Quieter." Now you know why she's always smiling.

With the sun going down on another idyllic Oshkosh evening, Steve and Suzanne point the Chipmunk back toward the Wittman Field where they will settle in for a quiet night of friends and fans sitting around the motor home campsite set up on the ramp of the Weeks hanger.

MICHAEL GOULIAN

If there were to be an ambassador of goodwill charged with promoting and forging a keen vision of the future for the airshow community, Michael Goulian cuts the ideal profile of such a figure. In this industry, Michael commands the highest respect of his peers as a pilot and possesses incredible professional intuition that keeps him at the top of this game year after year. With the birth of his daughter this season and an expanding role in the Red Bull Air Races, Michael Goulian has mastered the challenge of balancing business with pleasure by simply making it all about the fun.

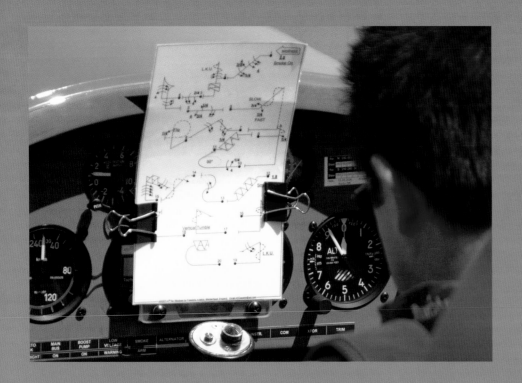

The Aresti card of aerobatic notations describes with symbols what Michael's routine looks like on paper. The powerful Lycoming Thunderbolt IO-580 easily pulls the new Extra 300SHP through knife-edge passes and will surely advance Michael in the Red Bull Air Races the next season. Previous page and opposite as seen from the Skymaster at Oshkosh.

Michael's "need for speed" is not limited to flying aerobatics! During the off season Mike plays competitive ice hockey twice per week, and skis with his airshow friends. In the summer, when he's not practicing or performing, he can be found improving his golf game. He is an avid F1 racing fan and if he could switch jobs with anyone in the world it would be with F1 driver, Juan Montoya.

His family founded one of the largest flying schools in the Northeast, Executive Flyers Aviation (EFA) in 1964. Michael learned the aviation business from the ground up by washing airplanes and sweeping the hangar floor. Being around airplanes at such a young age, Michael was bitten by the flying bug so it was only natural for Mike to learn to fly before he could even drive a car.

Michael started flying lessons in 1984 and soloed a Cessna 150 on his 16th birthday. Michael's yearning to fly aerobatics was so strong that he began his aerobatic training in 1985 while still a student pilot. Once he became and aerobatic instructor, Michael established an aerobatic school within EFA using a Decathlon trainer, and supplemented his income as a corporate jet pilot while working his way toward the top ranks of airshow display flying and competition aerobatics. Following a shower of regional titles he gained national recognition when at age 22 he became US National Champion in the Advanced Category. A year later he won the prestigious Fond du Lac Cup invitational competition and by 1992 he was the top ranked US male aerobatic pilot and Silver Medalist in the Unlimited Category, an achievement he repeated in 1993. His performance earned him a spot on the 1994

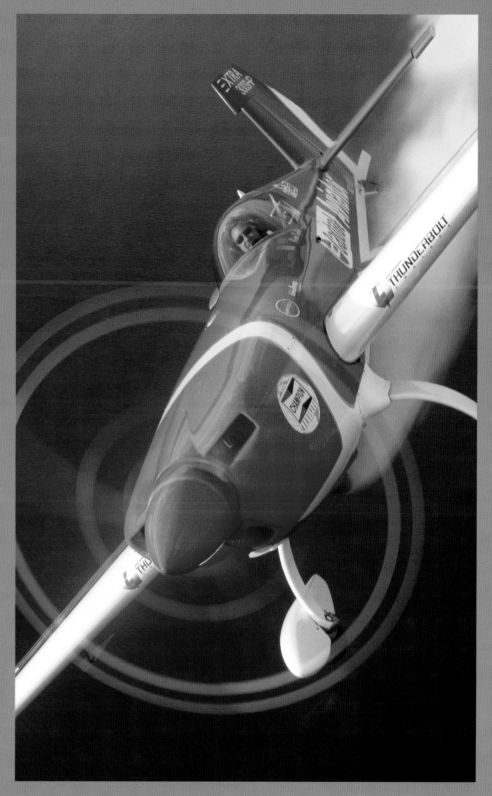

The suer-sleek lines of the all-new Extra 300SHP afford Michael not just more speed overall. it allows him more stability and control surface authority to execute maneuvers with increased precision and faster timing. Opposite page shows Michael over the lakes north of Oshkosh as the sun goes down and the shadows grow longer.

US National Aerobatic Team which represented America at the World Aerobatic Championship held in Hungary. In 1995 Mike reached the pinnacle of American aerobatics by becoming the US National Champion in the Unlimited Category. Not one to rest on his laurels, Mike has been a member of the 1994, 96, & 98 US Aerobatic Teams. Today, Mike focuses his attention on airshow flying and he is pushing the envelope with the goal of leading the industry to new heights entertainment and professionalism.

Aerobatics has been generous to Michael, and he feels a strong commitment to contributing to the future development of the sport. He is currently serving on the Board of Directors of the International Council of Airshows (ICAS), and supporting the International Aerobatic Club (IAC) by giving lectures to local chapters and promoting the regional aerobatic contests. He is also an Aerobatic Competency Evaluator, helping fledgling aerobatic performers launch their careers in airshow display flying. In 2003, Mike, along with Sean D. Tucker, mentored six future airshow pilots to kick off the new program, "Stars of Tomorrow", to introduce young talent to the Oshkosh AirVenture audience.

Michael is a perfectionist. This is proven by his attention to detail with maintaining his Castrol Aviator CAP232 showplane in top shape during the season (and sparkling with The Proper Aircraft cleaning products). Each winter the Castrol Aviator CAP 232 goes through a complete overhaul to ensure structural and mechanical integrity. Michael's performance in the air keeps its edge due to his fitness regimen throughout the year, spending time with a

coach to develop his own personal training routine.

Michael is coauthor of a series of best-selling aerobatic training books. Basic and Advanced Aerobatics have become the industry standard for aerobatic flight training manuals.

During his airshow career, Michael has developed a strong personality in the airshow community as one of the most approachable, likeable and professional performers on the circuit. Take time to meet Mike after any of his airshows this summer.

The increased roll rate of the Extra 300SHP is obvious in the sequence above. Opposite shows the big-bore Lycoming Thunderbolt engine up close and growling smoothly. GOULIAN 29

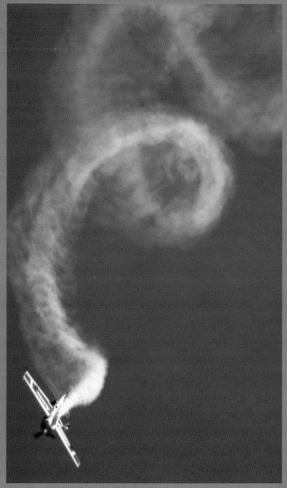

During the EAA Convention at Oshkosh and throughout the year for that matter, Michael relies heavily on his co-crew chiefs Mike Cappiello and Marcy Gruener both for ferrying the Extra and keeping her spotless and running smoothly.

The EXTRA 300SHP could provide Michael the maneuverability edge and the increased speed he needs to attain victory in the RED BULL AIR RACES this coming season.

JIM LeROY
BULLDOG AIRSHOWS

James Brown may have been the hardest working man in show business, but no one works harder in the airshow business than Jim LeRoy. An original one-man-band, "Bulldog" as he is known not only drives his family around the country from show to show in a specialized motorhome, he hauls the hangar along with them, assembling and breaking down his highly customized Pitts biplane at each venue... all by himself.

Starting down low and accelerating, Jim pulls back on the Bulldog and torque rolls skyward toward the Skymaster over the plowed fields near the Quad City Airshow. Previous page shows the Bulldog up close and personal. Opposite shows just how much Jim can clear the ribbon when he fly underneath before his knife-edge cut pass.

The recipient of the 2002 Art Scholl Showmanship Award and the 2003 Bill Barber Award for Showmanship, Jim is one of only eleven performers ever to receive both of these highly prestigious honors. His entertaining flying style coupled with his dynamic personality and tireless energy has made Jim one of the most recognized performers in the history of the business. Jim is one of only a handful of full-time "stunt pilots" in the world and actually makes his living by performing for airshow audiences, world-wide. Because of his dedication and commitment to excellence, Jim has established himself as one of the busiest and most sought after airshow performers in the industry today.

Jim, a former Marine Corps Scout/Sniper, holds a B.S. degree in Aeronautical/Aerospace engineering as well as an Airframe and Powerplant (A&P) license. His list of pilot ratings includes single-engine, multi-engine, airplane instructor, helicopter, helicopter instructor, instrument instructor, and aerobatic competency evaluator.

Considered by many as the premier solo act in the business today, Jim LeRoy has pushed aerobatic flying to a new and unsurpassed level. With a routine full of signature maneuvers and heart-stopping surprises, Jim redefines the limits with explosive, non-stop action from start to finish. "People want to see low, wild, and seemingly out of control, but at the same time they want discipline, precision, and complete control" says Jim. "You've got to take all of those elements and fuse them together in just the right way".

Jim attacks the classic maneuvers with a "new age" energy,

While it looks like Jim is flying circles around the photo-ship, he is actually rock-steady here in a knife-edge. Opposite shows variation of the theme of inverted and cross-controlled positions that we used to capture the most dynamic and aggressive views of Bulldog I.

adds the state-of-the-art gyroscopic stuff, throws in some tricks of his own and combines it all into a mesmerizing display of aerodynamic dynamite that will leave even the most seasoned airshow spectators shaking their heads in amazement.

Jim has two show planes, Bulldog I and Bulldog II. The aircraft pictured in flight is Bulldog I. It is a highly modified Pitts S2S, and has been Jim's show plane since he started performing in 1994. Starting in 2007, Jim's primary show plane will be Bulldog II, a brand new, state-of-the-art Biplane designed and built by Kevin Kimball, Steve Wolf and the late Curtis Pitts. Bulldog I will be used for international venues and now sports its own shipping container complete with tools, spare motor, and other parts. "Having two complete airshow operations allows me to venture into other parts of the world – there are lots of shows and lots of adventures just waiting out there beyond our borders!" says Jim.

In 2002, Jim LeRoy co-founded X-Team.

"Airshows and airshow performers need to evolve!" If you ask Jim LeRoy what the industry needs to do to advance itself, this is what he will tell you. "All other types of entertainment have moved forward – sporting events, movies, theater, video games, you name it, and it's come a long way in the past two decades. Airshows, on the other hand, seem to be stuck in the 50's. In fact, I think we've gone backwards. Innovative and colorful barnstorming type acts have been replaced with sponsored mediocrity that is often free to the show but lacks the showmanship and entertainment

exhibited by our predecessors." In a time where crowds are down and losses are up, and the mid-size show seems to be on the endangered species list, his words ring true. "We, as an industry, need to stop doing the same thing over and over, wondering why we don't get better results, and start evolving and getting better at what we do —namely entertaining our crowds. If we don't entertain them someone else will – that's the nature of business and free enterprise."

In 2002, Jim LeRoy co-founded what many people in the business refer to as the biggest thing that's happened in the airshow business in a long, long time – the X-Team. From 2002-2005 the X-Team rocked the house with the "over the top" presentations of "CRITICAL MASS" and the "MASTERS OF DISASTER". In 2006, they introduced the extremely well received "TINSTIX of DYNAMITE". In 2007, they will push onward with TINSTIX, as well as a new version of the MASTERS OF DISASTER show called "CODENAME: MARY'S LAMB". Interesting names and top-name performers are trademarks of the X-Team. "Take a few solo performers and have them perform at any given airshow equates to a mere airshow lineup, but take those same solo performers, allow them to interact with each other on the stage at the same time, add a storyline, soundtrack, and special effects, and now you have a theatrical production, and in the airshow business that means evolution. There is nothing else in the business today that compares to an X-Team performance, just ask the audience."

Jim's wife Joanie turns the table on the photographer. Jim's knife-edge ribbon cut photo composite with two motordrive frames of the same pass. Jim does a near vertical take-off in less than 200 feet under the power of his LyCon built Lycoming engine. Opposite shows that you do not need a plane to get good airborne shots of the Bulldog.

With the introduction of Jurgis Kairys and Skip Stewart, Jim LeRoy's pet project Mary's Lamb has become the talk of the town. Together with master-blaster Rich Gibson of Rich's Incredible Pyro, the new tongue-in-cheek narrative and heart-stopping aerobatics will surely keep audiences on their feet. Bottom left was taken by Steve Schulte and the canopy to canopy pass with Skip Stewart was captured by Scott Slocum of AutoPILOT Magazine.

Top left shows the all new Bulldog II that will be Jim's primary performance airplane in the States while the original Bulldog is part of a self-contained traveling unit for his international shows. Jim and Jurgis making their own cloud layer as the sun comes up over Oshkosh. The unique anime' inspired artwork for both Tinstix and Mary's Lamb.

A quick visit to the X-Team website illustrates what Jim is talking about. The storyline is a futuristic, science fiction tale, based on actual current events. The world is a different place and the common man is oppressed by robotic machinery controlled by a vast network of artificial intelligence. There are Freedom Fighters using antiquated flying machines to defeat the more powerful enemy. These Freedom Fighters are led by a mysterious and powerful woman – referred to only as Mary.

"TINSTIX" and "CODENAME: MARY'S LAMB" are names that represent the military operations carried out by the Freedom Fighters in this fictional dark world. The airshow performances are portrayals of these same operations pulled right out of the storyline, and brought to life in front of live audiences every weekend. The impact is WOW and the result is evolutionary – well done X-Team.

So, what's next for Jim LeRoy – another type of act, another type of plane, or perhaps another X-Team show? "I'm not ruling anything out, but I think that my biggest contribution to the airshow business thus far has been my work with X-Team" says Jim. "80 years ago, people were amazed that airplanes flew. Later, they were amazed when airplanes flew upside down. _ Today, tricks in a solo performance just don't have the impact they once had no matter how good you are – people want to see more, and with all the elements contained in an X-Team show, we can give it to them."

Down low and hauling ass, Jim puts the Bulldog through it's paces at the Quad City Airshow. Opposite shows just how precisely Jim can fly with full right rudder and the throttle for control.

JOHN KLATT
AIR NATIONAL GUARD

Ask any pilot. They'll tell you exactly when they got bitten by the flying bug. For many of them, it was when they were a kid. They were probably standing at an airport and looking at an airplane with their mouth open when they said to themselves, "That's what I want to do."

Clockwise top left is Major Pat Freeman flying over Lake Superior in a Minnesota Air Guard F-16C. A C-130 from the St. Joseph Missouri Air Guard flies formation behind the lead Herc photo ship over the St. Joe countryside during a photo flight with John Klatt seen next over the Guard ramp. The famous lift bridge in Duluth passes below John and Pat. John Klatt pilots the Staudacher S-300 behind the open ramp of a Minnesota Air Guard C-130 photo ship that flew up from their base in Minneapolis for this photo mission of Lake Superior just north of the City of Duluth.

John Klatt and the Guarding America, Defending Freedom Aerobatic Team give that experience to tens of thousands of people every year. Jaws drop when John throws himself through super-human gyrations in his Staudacher S-300 with the roar of the engine and the smoke trailing behind. Who knows how many kids will grow up to spend a life in aviation because of this airshow demonstration? The Guarding America, Defending Freedom Aerobatic Team travels the country inspiring people of all ages and educating young people about how they too can pursue their future in the Air National Guard.

The Air National Guard

The Air National Guard is a reserve component of the United States Air Force. It was founded on the same day in 1947 that the Air Force became a separate service. Today, the Air National Guard is at the forefront for individuals who want to excel in the high-tech industries of the 21st century. Members receive comprehensive training in some of the most technologically advanced skills the military has to offer. The Air National Guard provides 188 career opportunities in a variety of fields, including communications, engineering, technology, and healthcare. There are over 140 Air Guard units throughout the U.S. and its territories.

Unlike other branches of the armed services, the Air National Guard serves a dual role, supporting both Federal and State missions. For States, the Air Guard answers the call of Governors in times of disaster such as hurricanes, forest fires, or other civil emergencies. The Air Guard's Federal mission is to answer the President's call for overseas humanitarian aid or combat in support of Homeland Defense.

Always smiling, John Klatt flashes V for Victory over weekend sailboats near Newport Rhode Island during the Ouonset Airshow hosted by the Rhode Island National Guard. A true family affair, John Klatt enlists his boy Danny to set the tail wheel chocks after a short taxi back from the runway during the Red Wing airshow in Minnesota with neighbor Jeff Salisbury.

Most Air National Guard members enjoy the advantage of serving part-time from their hometown. Part-time service allows them to lead normal lives, to pursue full-time careers, or to attend college full-time.

Today's guardsmen and women are your doctors, lawyers, police officers, cooks, teachers, and factory employees—workers both blue- and white-collar. Civilians in peace, airmen in war, the Air National Guard protects America's skies.

The Air National Guard offers many federal benefits and entitlements to members and their families, including up to 100% tuition assistance and student loan repayment. Other benefits include the Base Exchange, Commissary, and use of Morale Welfare and Recreation facilities, to name just a few. (To receive these benefits, members must enlist for a minimum of 6 years.) In addition to the federal benefits listed above, each state may offer additional benefits for their members, such as state tax deferment and reduced auto license fees. Visit www.GoANG.com to learn more.

The Airshow

The Guarding America, Defending Freedom Aerobatic Team puts on a show bound to appeal to all ages. John Klatt puts on a 10-minute hard core, high energy, unlimited aerobatic show that airshow crowds love. Here are some of the maneuvers that John performs in his Staudacher S-300: Snap rolls with multiple linked rolls in the opposite direction, shark's tooth with multiple rolls on the forty-five up line, outside half loop up with a tumble off the top, and pull to vertical multiple rolls followed by a knife edge spin. Then, like you'd expect from a Minnesota barnstormer, John does a maneuver with a "snow" theme called the "outside avalanche." These are just a few of the moves John demonstrates. You have to see this show to believe it.

The Airplane

The aircraft John Klatt flies for the Guarding America, Defending Freedom Aerobatic Team is special. It's the world famous Staudacher S-300D which was hand-crafted by John Staudacher in the Bay City area of Michigan. The Staudacher was built for world class unlimited aerobatics and has competed in several world contests in many foreign countries. The Staudacher is very light-weight and is built with an all tubular and wood makeup which allows the airplane to weigh in at 1250 pounds. The Staudacher is powered by a Lycoming AIO-540 engine delivering more than 330 horsepower and has the latest Wide Chord MT three-bladed propeller built to take the gyroscopic maneuvers that John flies for the crowd. The Staudacher has a specialty smoke system which turns a gallon a minute into fun for everybody at the airshow.

There are several associate sponsors that help this airplane and this team run smoothly. They include: Aeroshell, Superior Air Parts, Aircraft Tool Supply and Tempest. For additional information about John, his airshow schedule, and his aircraft, go to www.johnklattairshows.com.

The Air National Guard has a long list of airplanes in service. The Guard has bases all around the country that fly a variety of aircraft: C-130 Hercules, F-15 Eagle, A-10 Thunderbolt, C-5 Galaxy, KC-135 Stratotanker, HH-60 Pave Hawk and C-17 Globemaster. Go to www.GoANG.com to find out how to pursue a career as an officer and a pilot in the Air National Guard.

The opposite page shows John's wife, mom and two kids during his Oshkosh performance. Above you can see John as he flies for the huge crowds of Oshkosh and enjoys a parade before his fans from the back of the EAA Ford Mustang.

Passing over the ANG base at St. Joe with one of their C-130s in trail. Going vertical at Red Wing, and out over Lake Superior near his ANG base in Duluth. John man's up for a flight at Red Wing.

John with his brother Mark and his son Jonas have their photo taken after the Red Wing flight by Virge . John gets a kiss from his daughter Leah on his way out to fly for the Red Wing crowds. John climbs out after another dazzling performance in front of tens of thousands of Oshkosh fans. LtCOL. Pat Freeman over Lake Superior in a Duluth ANG Viper.

The Pilot

John Klatt listened to his father's aviation stories and decided to see what was possible. He got private pilot training in his teens and got his college education at the University of Minnesota-Duluth. Meanwhile, he earned advanced civilian pilot ratings while working for Dagnon Aviation in Lakeville, Minnesota. John earned a commission in the Air National Guard and flew C-130 Hercules aircraft in support of missions all around the globe. John currently serves in the 148th Fighter Wing in Duluth, Minnesota where he is a fighter pilot in the F-16 Fighting Falcon. He has over 1200 hours at the stick of the F-16. He has served honorably during combat sorties in Operation Iraqi Freedom and during air defense missions in support of Homeland Defense. John is a Major in the Minnesota Air National Guard with over 16 years of service.

As a parallel to his military aviation career, John began actively training for, and competing in aerobatics. He competed in numerous regional and national competitions and found a place in the unlimited class aerobatic arena. He brought home an impressive collection of wins and became recognized as one of the top ten unlimited class aerobatic pilots in North America. Aerobatics became a personally fulfilling and integral component of John's life. This passion for high-intensity flying comes through in every show with the Guarding America, Defending Freedom Aerobatic Team.

The Bottom Line

John is a devoted husband to Deborah and father to two delightful children. Whether he's flying over Iraq or show center at an airshow, John knows the reason behind what he's doing. He's serving his country in the Air National Guard and protecting families all across Minnesota and throughout the United States of America. Maybe there will be kids at an airshow who are inspired by John's aerobatics and choose a path into the Air National Guard like he did. Go see for yourself. You'll be glad you did.

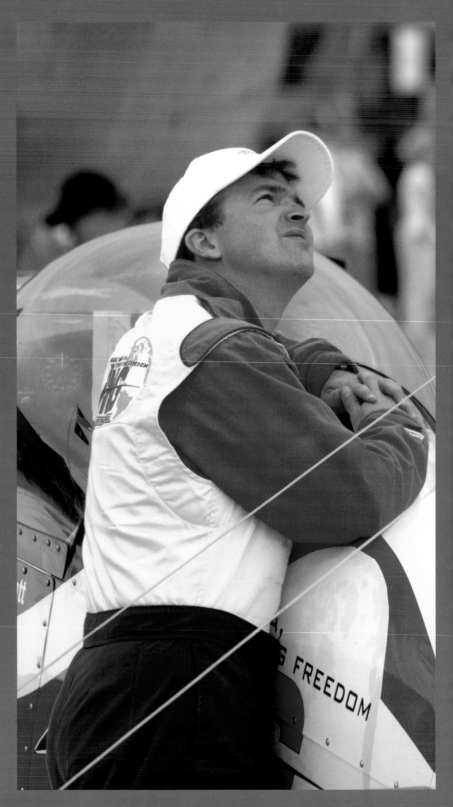

MICHAEL MANCUSO

with MATT CHAPMAN

There is nobody in this business with more airborne experience in unusual attitudes than Michael Mancuso. He made a name for himself as the gutsy slot pilot with the legendary Northern Lights 5-ship formation team, literally flying circles around team lead Andre Lortie and he has never looked back.

You can see from the images why Michael Mancuso is so famous for his inverted flight skills. Whether it is with Matt Chapman or solo over the Twin Beech, Mike is always rock solid. Previous page show the incredible never-before attempted photo formation we all dreamed up down in St. Pete during a series of photo flights with the Skymaster.

Always building on his experiences of being upside down when everyone else is shiny-side-up, Michael's performances continue to challenge the laws of gravity and conventions of formation aerobatics by inventing aerial presentations never before attempted by the rest of the airshow world.

Since going solo after the Northern Lights disbanded and went their own ways, Michael has diversified his showmanship skills with the opportunities that came with his six-year partnership with the legendary toolmakers Klein Tools. Beyond reaching millions of people annually flying airshows, Klein wanted to leverage the impact of Michael's low-level aerobatics in an all new arena of spectator sports: Indy Car racing. For the past four years, Michael Mancuso has been the centerpiece of Klein Tools cross-promotion marketing agenda that has saturated both the aviation and motor sports establishments through prime-time television broadcasts and as the official airshow of the Indy Racing League and the American leMans Series.

Klein Tools saw untapped marketing value in what Michael was doing in the airshow world and together, they developed and implemented a unique and hugely successful multi-dimensional program that has since been imitated but never equaled. To maximize his side of the program, Michael enlisted the help of long-time friend and fellow extreme aerobatic performer

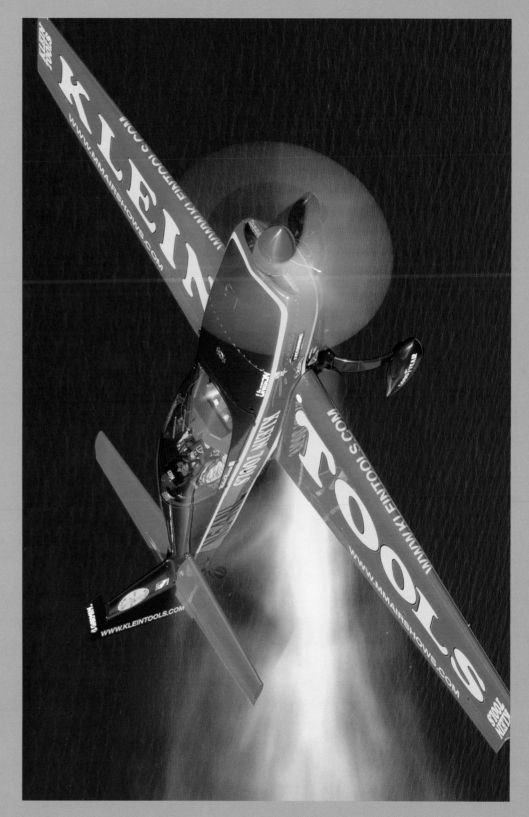

On these pages you see the classic lines of the Beech-18 over the Breakers, the famous stretch of tycoon mansions just east of Newport, RI. Quonset Point ANG LTC Dan Walter is treated to a grueling photo-mission formation flight and scores big points for keeping it tight. COL Mark Sheehan was driving the Skymaster.

Matt Chapman. Through hours and hours of practice and experimentation, these two incredible solo pilots melded their collective talents into a ten-minute performance that captivated and mesmerized crowds both at airshows and at car races alike. The genius of the pair's demonstrations was that because they were so good at flying together, they could maintain their formations in a compact aerobatic area defined by the smaller arenas found near race tracks or the urban venues otherwise off-limits to a conventional airshow performance.

The performances in front of the race crowds proved so successful that Klein Tools quickly had Michael flying more track demonstrations than airshows. Their brilliant vision for seeing the marketing synergy of combining Michael's aerial presentations with the entirely separate fan base of racing essentially more than doubled their penetration of the market and led to a whole new direction for Michael to explore with his flying. The opportunities for servicing corporate VIPs and the increased media attention at these expanded venues offered Michael the chance to fulfill a long time desire to acquire his now famous classic Beech 18, a 1940's era passenger plane reminiscent of Amelia Earhart's Lockheed Electra.

Empowered with the adrenalin-pumping power of his two-seat Extra 300 for the performances and a lucky few who are treated to an aerobatic

familiarization flight, Michael now has the added value of being able to offer first-class champagne sunset flights to prospective airshow clients as well as the many special people of interest that Michael wanted to pamper like his associate sponsors Lycoming, Garmin, Goodyear and Unison. The Twin Beech also serves as a wonderful support plane that can accommodate additional ground support personnel as well as parts and supplies typically needed during and airshow weekend. In the off-season, Michael is showing up in an increasing number of Hollywood blockbusters. He was granted membership in the coveted Screen Actors Guild for his role in Robert DeNiro's THE GOOD SHEPHERD in which he can be seen flying the Twin Beech.

On more than a few occasions, Michael generously treats military personnel from various Navy, Army or Air Force units to scenic pleasure flights as his way of thanking them not only for their hard work at the airshows but for their service to our country as well. All enjoy the chance to fly in a genuine WWII transport aircraft as this actual Twin Beech served under the C-45 designation during the war.

Due to his unusual cross-discipline marketing experience Michael enjoys a level of celebrity among his fans that rivals any rock-star. He spends countless hours connecting with his devoted followers along the crowd lines, in the pits and back in town even after the events are long over.

Out over Tampa Bay, Mike and Matt get in some late afternoon practice for the bridge commuters.

The transporter is a home away from home when Mike is on the road and treating his friends and sponsors to a first-class experience. Mike flies circles around Matt and a re dux of the maneuver first made famous with the Northern Lights.

Upside down is standard for Michael seen here over Newport Harbor. Matt and Mike facing the EAA parade of fame during Oshkosh week. Rob Reider speaks with Matt after his flight at one of the ACAP events.

Because of how much time he spends with folks on and off the clock, he has engineered one of the highest-class transporters in the industry that affords he and his team a place to escape the heat and pressures of such long hours under the summer sun. Both a sanctuary as well as a traveling billboard, the transporter concept originally developed on the racing circuits is now quickly catching on in the airshow world for all the same reasons. It saves on logistical expenses, local on-site rental costs and allows a level of brand continuity and luxury that all sponsors expect and recognize as valuable essentials to their marketing programs.

So while Michael Mancuso resides at the top tier of all sponsored airshow performers for his skill and showmanship, it is his marketing prowess and ever-evolving talent for being "the next big thing" that elevates him into the league of his own that seems to reflect his exact lifestyle and personal energy. That is why his charisma is so undeniable, because Michael Mancuso is the real deal.

Opposite page shows a frame from the opening sequence that is flipped vertically to demonstrate how bizarre a formation it really is. You cannot tell which way is up, and that is what makes these pilots so good.

PATTY WAGSTAFF

CIRRUS DESIGN

If the airshow world were a kingdom, then Patty Wagstaff would be the Queen. Her mass appeal and undisputable talent elevate Patty to the closest thing there is to aviation royalty. Few living aviators enjoy such universal celebrity and professional respect as the now platinum blonde aviatrix who has been inducted into the Aviation Hall of Fame and whose plane adorns the halls of the Smithsonian Air & Space Museum in our nation's capital.

Clockwise from top left: Patty's canine kids Cassidy and Ripley, both Jack Russel Terriers wait eagerly in the car for mom to return to earth. The Patty smile flashes for all her fans who turn out in droves at the chance to have their picture taken with her after trekking in from all over to see yet another live performance year after year. The previous and opposite pages show Patty giving the visitors to the Split Rock Lighthouse along the north shore of Lake Superior a show to remember.

It seems a theme among airshow pilots that parents provide the path to aviation. In Patty's case, it was her dad who was a Captain for Japan Air Lines and moved his family to the Far East when she was nine years old who first opened the door into the cockpit. When Patty was ten years old, she had her first experience at the controls of her dad's DC-6 and, as they say, the rest is history. But few aviators outside of lifelong military test pilots can rattle off a list of accomplishments as long as Patty Wagstaff, never mind female aviators.

Patty learned to fly in Alaska where becoming a pilot carries with it a unique set of skills not usually learned by students in the lower forty-eight. Short, narrow, uneven strips, low clouds, heavy rain, dead reckoning, glassy lakes, gusty wind and icing are all your instructors in Alaska, and Patty learned from the best. By the time she left Alaska, she enjoyed the experience of a pilot with three times as many hours. And so she flew on to the next adventure in aviation that led her to aerobatics, where she could hone her stick and rudder prowess into razor sharp maneuvers and earn a name among the best in the world.

Patty Wagstaff excelled in aerobatic competitions, reaching the pinnacle of international Olympic-level ranks, winning a gold medal as well as silver and bronze along the way. In America, Patty was the first woman to earn the title of US National Aerobatic Champion and among an elite few pilots to have done it three times. But once again, reaching the summit in the world of

Blurring the birch and aspen woods near Gooseberry Falls on the great North Shore of Lake Superior, Patty drives toward the shore in her Extra 300. Opposite page shows a wider shot of the beauty and splendor of Split Rock Lighthouse and the surrounding North Woods region home to Cirrus Design.

competitive flying simply led Patty to her next challenging adventure in aviation. The precision of aerobatic competition for the sake of points and of judging, while personally exhilarating, lacked a sense of showmanship. Patty had flown a few aerobatic performances in front of public crowds as part of her experiences competing for the US National Championships, and the feedback afforded by fans on the ground struck a chord in Patty that was irresistible.

After claiming victory to all that could be achieved, Patty retired from competitive aerobatics to focus on adapting her repertoire of eye-watering maneuvers inside the judging box into a knee-weakening airshow routine along the crowd line. Every airshow pilot has a style and look to their performances, and Patty's is among the most recognizable. Where most pilots make their mark with either shock or beauty, Patty somehow has tamed raw aggression with just enough feminine refinement that she draws in the entire spectrum of the airshow crowd. By doing so, she is able to tap an incredible source of fan-based adulation. Whether you are an actor on a stage or a trapeze artist in the big top, all performers crave the same thing: appreciation of their craft. Patty Wagstaff has mastered the art of wooing the crowd, and the crowd has clearly wooed Patty in return.

Besides the affection of fans around the world, Patty Wagstaff caught the attention of aviation industry giants for the incredible precision of her flying and the remarkable depth of her experience. Raytheon hired

her as their test and demonstration pilot for the new joint US Air Force and Navy primary trainer, the T-6 Texan II which afforded her opportunities to travel overseas to world aviation showcases like the Farnborough Airshow.

Most recently, pioneering aircraft manufacturer Cirrus Design, based in Duluth, Minnesota, enlisted Patty as their officially sponsored airshow representative to travel the country not only to build brand recognition, but to build time in their flagship SR22 design. In between performances, she pilots her own SR22 which is the company's coveted 2000th production aircraft. By growing her Cirrus-specific experiences she is developing an increased technical perspective that offers the company valuable insights on performance strategies that may improve on the already wildly popular innovations found in the best selling aircraft in the world.

The story of Cirrus Design starts with Alan and Dale Klapmeier, two brothers from DeKalb, Illinois. In 1984 they founded Cirrus Design to manufacture and distribute their home-build airplane kit called the VK-30, a sleek tapered-winged craft that featured a v-tail and a pusher prop. Designing and selling the experimental aircraft served as an ideal laboratory that developed their skills for engineering innovative solutions to the standard set of challenges facing all aircraft manufacturers. Like the Rutan brothers further west in the Mojave desert, the Klapmeier boys chose to pioneer new manufacturing techniques and processes to suit their unique vision of

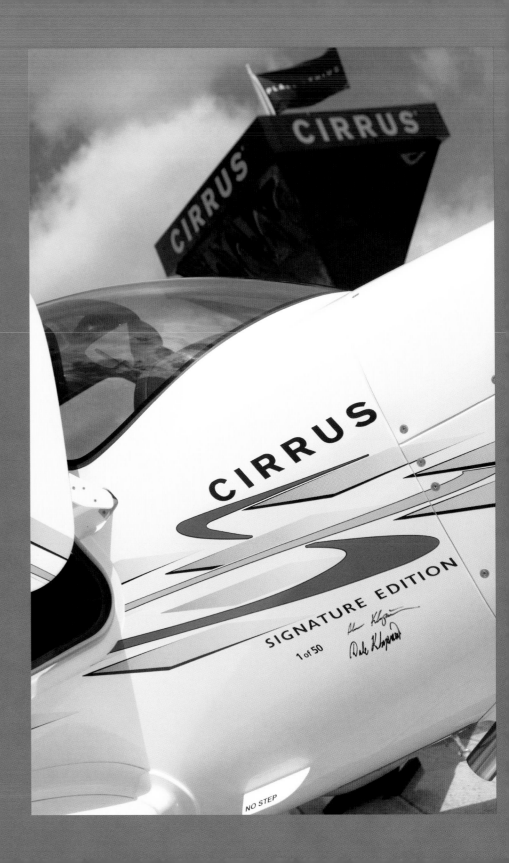

As evidence of their significance in the aviation universe, the Cirrus Design Village at Oshkosh served as Mecca for all flying Pilgrims seeking enlightenment or simply a glimpse the Queen. The opposite page shows one of the special limited edition production aircraft that has helped Cirrus Design continue to increase market share.

Wowing the crowd during the Monaco Airshow in Duluth. When Patty is not flying, she can often be found harnessing the power of a single horse near her home in St. Augustine, Florida. Airshow fan #1 Denise Decker took the photo of Patty in the paddock.

Clockwise from top left: Inverted and loving it over the show line at the Monaco Airshow in Duluth. Strapping in for another performance, you can clearly she her scripted pictograph of the flight called an Aresti card named for the Spanish Count credited with inventing the notation system. Over the Split Rock Lighthouse on Lake Superior near the headquarters of Cirrus Design.

what an airplane ought to be rather than simply update the existing concepts of what a light plane was already.

Parlaying their experiences with the VK-30, Dale and Alan set out with determination rivaling the Wright brothers to design and produce an all-composite certified general aviation aircraft, and they did it in the relative backwaters of northern Minnesota. Within ten years, the first prototype had been flown, and soon after they were ramping up full scale production in a newly expanded facility at Duluth International Airport.

Today, Cirrus Design has delivered over 3,000 aircraft worldwide as they continually introduce highly desirable and market-snatching innovations like air conditioning, turbo-charged performance and creative limited edition trim packages. The SR line of aircraft is now and has been the best selling type in the world, which is an accomplishment as impressive as the plane itself. By ignoring conventional schools of design and manufacturing, positively engaging the daunting FAA certification process and listening to their highly skilled employees and suppliers, Cirrus Design has inspired a whole new genre of aviation enthusiast. It is now easy to see why they have partnered with Patty Wagstaff, because inspiration is what drives innovation. Watching Patty perform all season long and rubbing elbows with her fans is a renewable source of inspiration, and like everything else at Cirrus Design, they have cornered the market.

Skidding her Extra 300 over Lake Superior, Patty chases the Skymaster photo ship through the waning evening sunlight. Opposite page shows Patty in her dedicated commuter, Cirrus Design's 2000th production aircraft, N2000M that she flies to and from each airshow.

ED SHIPLEY
JIM BEASLEY
P-51 HORSEMEN

If there were ever two guys that had more fun flying two of the coolest fighters ever built, I'd like to meet them. As it stands, Ed Shipley and Jim Beasley routinely transform that joy into a level of precision formation aerobatics unrivaled by any other Mustang pilots around the world. In his spare time Ed Shipley has dreamed up and launched AIR SHOW BUZZ.com, a killer website community dedicated to all of us who live for this stuff.

AIRSHOWBUZZ
★com

Seen here during the Dayton Air Show, the normally two-ship Horsemen routine was augmented by stick-and-rudder legend Snort Snodgrass.

INTRODUCING WWW.AIRSHOWBUZZ.COM

Do you fly in your dreams? Who among us has not daydreamed of soaring through the skies as a fighter pilot, a barnstormer or even as the captain of a 747. The public's fascination for flight found a new home in www.airshowbuzz.com. Designed by air show industry insiders for those who are passionate about air shows and all things aviation, AirShowBuzz filled a void for those seeking to share their aviation stories from around the world through videos, photos and forum discussions.

It is the only site where you'll find the Raptor Demo pilot and three time national aerobatic champion, Patty Wagstaff both answering the fans' questions directly, as well as sharing their own stories. Because of its unique group of founders, ASB also allows aviation enthusiasts to step beyond the crowd line into the cockpit of some of the world's top air show performers and military demos through their exclusively produced videos.

The founders of ASB are as diverse as their site: Ed Shipley, ICAS Board member and air show performer, Stephanie Ross-Simon; a Hollywood script writer and promotions expert, Deb Mitchell, former ICAS VP and director of NAS Oceana's air show, General (retired) Hal Hornburg, former commander of USAF's Air Combat Command, and Jim Beasley, an attorney, doctor, air show performer and owner of several P-51 Mustangs.

ASB is truly the who's who of aviation.

KIRBY
CHAMBLISS
RED BULL EDGE

In recent years, the airshow universe experienced a super nova expansion that is the Red Bull Air Racing series. This worldwide aviation spectacle is an adrenalin junkies dream and at the top of the race standings soars Kirby Chambliss in his Red Bull Edge 540.

After flying in front of the huge crowds of the Quad City Airshow in Davenport, Iowa, Kirby took the Red Bull Edge 540 up over the farm fields for a photo mission with his Beech Baron support plane.

Some people build their dream home on a golf course. Kirby Chambliss built his on a runway. "My hangar is part of my house, and I can fly upside down right past my door," says the genial Texas native. It's all part of being one of the best aerobatic pilots the United States has ever known.

Chambliss is captain of the U.S. Aerobatics Team, and he's a rare five-time winner of the National Aerobatic Championship, which equates to second most titles on the all-time list. One of the ways he stays in peak form for the demands of competition is by performing in airshows around the world, and in a new Red Bull Edge 540 plane, Chambliss is bringing his heart-stopping feats to more fans than ever before.

Commercial Pilot and Champion Pilot.

From the time he was a child in Corpus Christi, Texas (where he was born in 1959), Chambliss wanted to be a pilot. His father taught skydiving, and young Kirby loved to ride along. His favorite part was when the pilot would race the skydivers back to the ground by putting the plane into a steep spiral.

In high school, Chambliss earned extra money as a lineman, fueling aircraft. He began formal flight training in 1979, and by December the 20-year-old soloed for the first time, earning his private license the following March. Chambliss worked as a certified flight instructor and then as a night freight pilot, but it was taking aerobatic training for a job flying a business jet that inspired him to save up for an aerobatic plane of his own.

In 1985 Chambliss bought a Pitts S2A and started rigorous aerobatic training. In his very first contest, he won top honors in the intermediate category, and he rapidly worked his way

Kirby slips the Red Bull Edge 540 in behind the Baron with smoke appearing out from under the painted flames on the cowling. Opposite shows Kirby's trademark Cobra takeoff. Breathtaking power.

up to the elite "unlimited" level. Chambliss was first named to the U.S. Aerobatic Team in 1997, and since then, he has taken four U.S. National Aerobatic Championships (including three consecutive from 2002-2004), as well as a variety of medals at the World Championships. In 2000, he was crowned Men's Freestyle World Champion.

Athlete and Showman.
Today, Chambliss is at the top of his game. He has earned virtually every license that aviation has to offer, he's flown more than 60 types of airplanes, and he's logged more than 24,000 hours (nearly three years!) in the air. And, he says, he's still learning.

"We do things in aerobatics now that would have broken an airplane five or six years ago," Chambliss comments. "Sometimes I land and think, 'How did that plane take it?'" He chuckles and adds "Of course, we pilots have the same bodies as always, and we have to take it!'"

What Chambliss and his airplane have to withstand is a span of 18 G's. Propeller planes, unlike jets, can handle negative G's, and the Zivko Edge 540 can go from negative 8 to positive 10. Chambliss likens the craft to "a rocket with wings." While only a few years ago it was impressive for a plane to turn end-over-end just once, these days pilots can tumble half a dozen times before pulling out. It's an incredible test of timing, concentration, and courage – not to mention stamina. To stay in shape, Chambliss runs and lifts weights, in addition to flying aerobatics three times a day, four days a week.

Outside of training and aerobatic competitions, Chambliss doesn't have any trouble impressing crowds when he performs at traditional airshows throughout the year. However, now that he has partnered with Red Bull, he'll also be entertaining at non-traditional events. "I'll be performing at all types of events, like a wakeboard competition, for example," he notes.

Having enjoyed flying in locations from Mexico and Hawaii to Europe and Asia in the past, Chambliss especially enjoys competing in the Red Bull Air Race World Series, a new aerobatic air racing series with rounds in several countries. Kirby finished the 2005 Red Bull Air Race World Series in third place overall. He took second at the stops in Longleat, U.K., Budapest, Hungary, and final in San Francisco where a time penalty cost him the race win.

In-between events, the personable pilot enjoys coming back home to Flying Crown Ranch, Arizona to his wife and fellow pilot, Kellie and their baby Karly Nicole.

The Red Bull Air Race World Series

Concept:

The Red Bull Air Race World Series is all about high-speed precision flying. The pilots each fly one at a time through a slalom-like race track of 50-foot air-filled pylons and pilots are penalized with added time if they fly to low or high through the pylons or touching a gate. The overall fastest aggregate time from each of the two final rounds on race day is the winner. This first-ever air race World Series is like any other motorsports series, such as NASCAR or F1, the pilots collect points through the season to determine the overall Red Bull Air Race World Series champion.

Crew Chief Jason Resop communicates with Kirby via handheld from the hot ramp at Quad Cities. Where there's smoke, there's fire... Jet truck Shockwave provides both as Kirby arcs overhead.

Life on the road is a family affair with wife Kellie and their baby Karly Nicole. Len Rulason leads the Red Bull support crew that keeps the plane in tip-top shape and ferries it from site to site while Kirby hauls the family around in the Baron.

Format:
The qualifying happens the day before the race where the running order for the following day is determined. The fastest pilot on qualifying day flies last on Saturday, whereas the slowest timed pilot flies first.

On race day, the first of the two rounds determines the running order for the second, final round. These two times on Saturday are combined and the fastest time wins with the winner collecting six points, second is awarded five, third place receives four and so on.
Competitors:

There are fourteen pilots competing in the 2007 Red Bull Air Race World Series. They are all world or aerobatic champions because such fast, efficient flying is required.

There are three American pilots; Kirby Chambliss the five-time and current U.S. Aerobatic Champion, Mike Mangold, was the series champion last year and Mike Goulian, a rookie in 2006.

Race History:
The Red Bull Air Race World Series was a concept developed by Red Bull and Hungarian pilot Peter Besenyei, who also competes in the series. The first race took place in 2001 in Zeltweg, Austria and in 2004 it made its U.S. debut at the National Championship Air Races in Reno, Nevada. Now in its fifth season, the global series makes twelve stops on multiple continents during the 2007 season.

On the flight back to the Quad Cities airport Kirby scoots low over the trees

USAF F-22 RAPTOR

The F-22 Raptor is an aircraft for its time. When just about everything is getting an "X" or "Extreme" attached to it, the Raptor defines the standard. Everything about it is extreme: performance, technology, capability, agility, expense, controversy.

– Essay by David C. Nilsen

All of these images were made during a single photo mission with a dedicated crew of USAF and civilian Heritage Flight players flying behind a C-130J out of Keesler AFB flown by Maj Dave Borsi. The unprecedented flight originated out of Tyndall AFB in Florida. The F-22 is flown by Maj Thomas Shank and Ed Shipley is flying Crazy Horse, the TF-51 Mustang trainer from Lee Lauderback's Stallion 51 operation in Kissimee, FL.

The Air Force calls it an "air dominance" fighter. The name says it all. Built to be the greatest fighter in the world to allow the United States to dominate its superpower adversary in the Cold War, the F-22 compromised on nothing. It has it all: stealth, advanced agility, supercruise, sophisticated electronics and avionics, thrust-vectoring engines, a thrust-to-weight ratio of 1.16:1. Its advanced Pratt & Whitney F119 engines can push it to Mach 1.5 without using afterburners ("supercruise") and well beyond that with afterburners. Its advanced flight controls and thrust vectoring engines make it one of the few aircraft in the world able to perform such maneuvers as "Pugachev's Cobra," the "Kulbit" (think of the Cobra, but the pitch continues all the way around like a reverse somersault), and to maneuver at extreme angles of attack from -40 degrees to over 60. Such agility leaves airshow crowds shaking their heads.

The Raptor (originally called "Lightning II" until 1997) carries its armament internally, to preserve its stealthy profile. Its three internal bays carry up to six AMRAAM and two Sidewinder missiles, or two 1000-pound bombs or 8 250-pound small diameter bombs instead of four AMRAAMs. These missiles are controlled by a "first-look, first-kill" fire control system that amassed an impressive 108:0 kill:loss ratio in a 2006 exercise against F-15s and F-16s.

But in a world with only one superpower, some say that the F-22 is too much of a good thing. In "the Long War," the Raptor has no real opponent. All that extreme capability comes at a high cost. The F-22 is the most expensive fighter in history, with a fly-away cost of $120 million per aircraft, or $361 million each when you factor in its development costs. And with high cost comes decreased production runs—originally 750 planned, now down to 183—which only drives costs farther up. The Air Force has fought a long battle to justify the F-22. In 2002 it renamed it the F/A-22 to make it seem more relevant in the Global War on Terror (it renamed it F-22 in 2005). Lately the Air Force is touting the Raptor as an intelligence, surveillance, and reconnaissance (ISR) platform—albeit a really fast, maneuverable and expensive one—which could be used to detect improvised explosive devices (IEDs) on Iraqi roads. Such has become the life of the air dominance fighter.

It is a measure of the change in the times, of the ratio of aerodynamic-technical advancement to political necessity, that the F-22 has taken more time—14 years—to advance from prototype selection (April 1991) to initial operational capability in December, 2005 than the B-17 was in production from prototype selection to end of production (1935–45). But it is also a measure of the Raptor's extreme capability that at the end of that time, it was not an antique like the B-17 in 1945, but still the hottest rod on the block. That's extreme.

Maj Thomas Shank leads the gaggle in the Raptor as Dale Snodgrass flies his F-8b Sabre with Lt Col Jerry Kerby in the F-4 Phantom and Maj Bret Anderson cracking the whip in the F-15C. RAPTOR 103

US NAVY BLUE ANGELS

SIXTY YEARS OF AVIATION DIPLOMACY

Teamwork defines the Blue Angels and is the single most important aspect of the squadron. The team is made up of 15 different job skills that must come together to form a self-contained unit. Team members must be willing to perform more than their share of the workload. Support officers often work outside their area of expertise, and crosstraining among enlisted team members is essential. The Blue Angels maintain a rigorous show schedule and deploy to each show with a minimum number of personnel — flexibility and teamwork is the key to success.

—Essay by David C. Nilsen

Top Left: Riding with LCDR Ted "Bunza" Steelman during the solo circle and arrive maneuvers at Quad Cities, we go head to head with #6 LCDR John Allison. The same maneuver during the demo the next day. A cool shot of Bert and the Delta during a Pensacola photo mission trying to line up the two elements with the lighthouse near the Blues hanger. Not that easy. Opposite page shows us inverted and heading down hill chasing the Delta loop with Loni Anderson. Previous page is a cool view of the Diamond pass looking through the 4-ship with all pilots visible wearing the alternate Gold flight suits. Bert inbound on the high-speed flat pass.

It's not just about the flying.

It's about everything they do. German-American architect Ludwig Mies van der Rohe famously observed, "God dwells in the details," and that is a point not lost on those who work in high-performance aviation. An almost infinite number of little things have to go right, *all the time*, to allow six blue-and-gold aircraft to fly at 400 miles per hour with only 36 inches separating each plane's wingtip from the wingtip or canopy of the next plane. It takes the best efforts of every one of the 125 members of the US Navy Flight Demonstration Squadron to allow the almost 70 shows that the "Blues" fly each year.

But it's still not just about the flying.

It's about the meaning of what they do, which is subconsciously evident to everyone who sees them turn four or six individual aircraft into one single object looping and rolling and careening through the skies. "Teamwork" is the word that we would try to use for this, but that word wilts before the reality of what they accomplish twice per weekend every weekend of the spring and summer. One is left groping for words like, "forge," as in forging steel, "integrate," as in integrity, unify, unity, united, and as it turns out, the answer is in your pocket—on each and every coin and dollar bill—the motto of this nation: *e pluribus unum*. "From many, one." Teamwork, unity, integrity. The Blue Angels are about America.

So it really is about more than just the flying.

And you can see it in everything they do. If you go to see the Blues at an airshow, and you're not sitting near show center, from where you can see the ground crew perform their proud ballet of service, you are missing the show. Yeah, the stuff in the air is great, but you're missing the show. Watch how the canopies go

The upper sequence composite from Loni's backseat chase depicts the same maneuver shown in the lower frames shot from the ground. We had to tuck and roll right after these frames... big could be heard all around. Opposite page shows us chasing the Diamond during their opening takeoff burner loop. Look back at the Double Farvel with the Lighthouse. Line abreast loo

up and down and the same instant, how the launch crew pull the chocks at precisely the same moment, how the crew chiefs work with the pilots to check the controls. See how as their jobs are done, the mechanics stand and run down the flightline in pure straight lines punctuated by crisp corners. Watch the snap and trust and pride in the salutes between the crew chiefs, line chief and the precisely taxiing pilots. And feel the handshakes the pilots share with their groundcrew when they deplane at show's end. If you miss that, you miss it all. And don't miss the way the ground crew arrives in their column of locally-rented sedans and minivans—in a high speed bumper-to-bumper caravan racing down the flightline, scarcely more than 36 inches between successive vehicles. The Blue Angel ground crew drive like the Blue Angel pilots fly.

Have you ever heard someone say they've got the weight of the world on their shoulders? That's the way people move, and stand when they have the weight of the world on their shoulders: Proud. Smart. Crisp. Because they know they're part of something bigger than themselves which is worth every exertion they can possibly make.

And you still haven't seen all of it. You haven't seen the flight surgeons, the admin personnel, the supply clerks. Of the 125 team members, only about 45 accompany the seven demonstration pilots and narrator to each show. It takes a lot of unsung heroes to make a blue delta in the sky. But they all know that it's worth it, and there's nothing else they'd rather do. And we who watch the fruits of their labors know in our gut that they're right.

The US Navy's Blue Angels are the oldest official military flight demonstration team in the world. 2006 was the 60th Anniversary of their setting the unsurpassed standard of excellence the world over for precision flying, for the beauty of human technical achievement, and for the pride that comes from seeing it all made real.

These frames show several moments of action during the demo that add to the dynamic nature of the Navy demonstration. Opposite page shows us chasing the Delta loop over the top. Top right is a fleeting snapshot that echoes the tail graphics on Bert during a home Wednesday practice.

As the Diamond burner loop climbs away from Earth, the solos take position on 25 Right and ready for blastoff. Opposite is a cool view over Loni's left shoulder of *b as he touches down and the rest of the Team rolls out after the PUB (pitch up break) shown above that.

The Blues were brought into existence by Fleet Admiral Chester W. Nimitz, victor of the Pacific War, in an April 24, 1946 directive. The Navy, knowing that Nimitz was not to be trifled with, wasted no time. Less than two months later, on June 15, the team performed its first show at Naval Air Station Jacksonville, their first home. The team at that time comprised four Grumman F6F-5 Hellcat fighters, like Nimitz, proud victors of our recent enemies and one SNJ Texan trainer. The Hellcats performed looping and rolling maneuvers in a three-ship Vee formation, while the fourth performed solo maneuvers, including simulated dogfights with the lowly SNJ, painted yellow and red to resemble a Japanese Zero of the recent war. A crewman in the backseat would even throw out a mannequin in a parachute as the "Zero" feigned crashing behind a convenient copse of trees.

But the team had no name. Half-heartedly called the "Lancers" or "Blue Lancers" for about a month, the team on a trip to New York came across an advertisement for a famous New York nightclub: The Blue Angel. They announced their new name on 19 July 1946. The rest is poetry.

All Blue Angels are volunteers. They are not assigned to the organization by the mysteries of the Navy's personnel system. Being a Blue Angel is not a just a job, it is a goal. They apply. They request the privilege and compete to be chosen as one of the select few who call themselves Blue Angels. They do not get paid any extra for what they do. They do it because they believe in it, and because they love it. Blue Angel #1, "Boss," is chosen by the Chief of Naval Air Training. Blue 1 must have at least 3000 hours in tactical jets, and have commanded a tactical jet squadron. The remaining pilots, and every other member of the team, are chosen by the team itself in a strenuous screening process. All applicants must be oriented toward a Navy career, and meet a variety of standards suited to their positions. Blue Angels 2-7 must be Navy or Marine Corps carrier-qualified jet

pilots with at least 1250 hours in tactical jets, and #8, the Events Coordinator must be a back-seater with the same qualifications. The Marine Corps pilots flying the C-130 support aircraft must be qualified as aircraft commanders with at least 1200 hours. Enlisted personnel are recommended by their current commanders, and be interviewed by all seven departments and 15 work centers of the squadron. Applicants are chosen by vote of the current team; pilots and officers require a *unanimous* vote. When a Blue Angel is chosen, that individual is expected to perform not only in his or her own professional area, but to be cross-trained in other skills to become part of the fabric of flawless excellence that the Blue Angels have woven. In their 60-year history, the Blue Angels have never cancelled an airshow due to a maintenance problem. That's why the ground crew are part of the demonstration, because without them, there is no demonstration. There are 125 Blue Angels; six of them happen to fly jets. So it's not just about the flying.

Blue Angels serve 2-3 years with the team (demonstration pilots generally serve two years), and then return to the Fleet, to continue their impeccable service to the nation. But it is a point of Blue Angel honor and pride that, "Once a Blue Angel, Always a Blue Angel."

After only ten shows in the Hellcat, the Blues switched to the F8F-1 Bearcat in 1946. In 1949, they entered the jet age, with the straight-winged F9F-2 Panther. In 1950, the Korean War interrupted, and the Blue Angels went to war. They repainted their jets in tactical markings and the Navy formed a new squadron, VF-191, "Satan's Kittens," around the Blue Angels core with the Blues Flight Leader, LCDR Johnny Magda, as the squadron commander. They went to war aboard USS *Princeton*. LCDR Magda was killed in combat over Korea. He would not be the last Blue Angels "Boss" to die in combat. And to this day the Blue Angels are still capable of making their jets combat ready within 72 hours and going to war.

Some try to compare the teamwork of military organizations like the Blue Angels to professional sports teams. But the comparison is not apt. The quality of a sports team rises and falls based on the persons filling various key roster or coaching spots. When a team wins a national championship twice in

The shot above is taken while inverted looking through the top of the canopy back at the Delta loop with the Blue Angel ramp visible at the bottom left. Opposite page is the backside of the Diamond loop with throttles at idle and boards out. Notice all the downed pine trees in the woods near the field that were blown down during the direct hit by Hurricane Ivan.

Always having a good time, the Blues are six guys at the top of their game, doing exactly what they always dreamed of and what they will remember for the rest of their lives. Whether one of the pilots, or one of the hundred or so ground support personnel, being a Blue Angel is as good as it gets in the Navy and it bodes very well for your career after leaving the Blue Angel family. Once Blue Angel, forever a Blue Angel.

BLUE ANGEL AIRLINES
FAT ALBERT

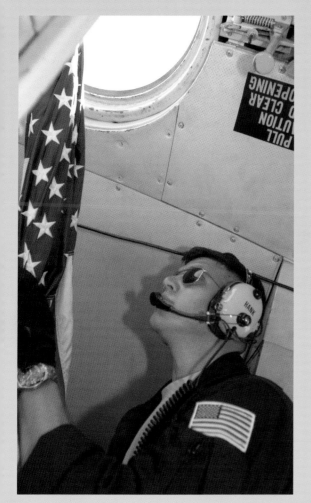

Opposite: Bert inbound on the high-speed flat pass. The series above chronicles the view from the flight deck during Bert's JATO Demo at Quad Cities. Clockwise from top left SSGT. Mike Wason stows Ol' Glory. 45 degrees from level. Rabbit hauls Bert around for the high-speed flat pass. Maj. Stefan "Hans" Mueller and Capt. Russ "Rabbit" Campbell: keep reaching for the rainbow guys. BLUES 119

a row, people wonder if they'll become "a dynasty," i.e., winning the championship three times in a row. Neither phenomenon has anything to do with the Blue Angels. First, there are no stars or marquee players on the team. The team's ability to perform is not based on the unique talents of any one non-reproducible individual. Their uncompromising excellence is produced by a team that changes every year, and must be constantly reforged with new members. The Blues do not achieve perfection because some of their individual members "are the best." The Blues achieve perfection because their individual members come together to become the best. Their demonstrations drive this point home. The uniformed pilots man their aircraft with smooth, easy precision. They shake hands, they salute. The only way to tell them apart is when the narrator announces their names and hometown. When they are in the air, they are referred to by their aircraft numbers. There is no high-fiving, head-butting, nor endzone histrionics. They are not showing off; they are pursuing perfection, and perfection doesn't care who you are, it only cares how hard you and your teammates work.

Second, the Blues' object is not beating a rival team, or winning a championship, but to achieve perfection each and every time out. Sports teams face better or worse opponents, but perfection and the laws of physics do not change. This is why the Blues do not have a back-up pilot. To do what they do safely, you cannot drop in a substitute. The high-level of intuitive teamwork that their jobs require does not allow it. From 1946 to 2006, twenty-five Blue Angels have lost their lives in flying accidents. Their standard of perfection is hard and uncompromising.

Finally, and this is not trivial, they really are role models. In this age of "I don't wanna be no role model," the Blues deliberately present themselves as role models. They visit schools and hospitals, they say, "if you join the Navy, you could do my job someday." You could be a pilot, you could work on jet aircraft, you could

organize deployments, you could support the personnel, for the best team in the world. "The best is not something you watch on TV. The best is in your grasp: you can join the best."

There is a reason why the Super Bowl begins with a Blue Angels fly-over, and airshows don't begin with a bunch of football players and their agents bickering over incentive clauses.

In 1951 the Navy reformed the Blues around former team members from "Satan's Kittens," and their demonstrations resumed in 1952. In 1955 the Blues unveiled their swept-wing F9F-8 Cougars, and in 1957 they moved into the supersonic F11F Tiger. They stayed in the Tiger for 11 years, and made a European tour with the Tiger in 1965. Flying at the Paris Airshow, along with several other national teams including the Air Force's Thunderbirds, the Blues earned the show's only standing ovation. In recognition of this unique achievement, the team was honored on the floor of the US Congress, and by the awarding of Distinguished Flying Crosses and Air Medals to the team.

In their pre- and postflight walkdowns, the Blues, like a magician, show us the tools they are about to use to amaze us. While they don't say, "nothing up my sleeve," they do show us that the same people get into and come back out of the amazing machines. Some spectators may wonder why they see the pilots attired only in knife-creased jumpsuits, and not the G-suits they would expect for use in high-performance jets. The walkdown shows us that the Blues don't wear G-suits. The tight formations and precise maneuvering flown by the Blues require a solid and steady hand on the flight control stick. The Blues use a technique of bracing their right arms against their thighs to gain the sort of leverage and steadiness they need, and the constant inflation and deflation of a G-suit's bladders would prevent this. Blues pilots withstand the significant G-pressures of their maneuvers by knowing what to expect and using muscle contractions to

2006 was the last year to witness the blast of a C-130 JATO takeoff. Clockwise from top left. JATO solid rocket fuel boosters. A photo composite of the tactical short field landing... very impressive from the ground, but the view from the cockpit as the windscreen fills up with Earth really get's your attention. Go Gumby GO!.

Rabbit briefs the flight at Quad Cities in the shade under the tail of Bert.. Getting ready to crank up. Fleeting JATO Magic: Photo by BA PA shooter Ryan Courtade. The local Marine color Guard for the Quad Cities airshow. Opposite: Bert hauling ass on the low transition takeoff at Quad Cities as the gear doors close.

hold the blood in their heads, a technique taught to all pilots. Like any magic trick, it's easy to know the secret. The trick is in taking all of the secrets, all of the details, and doing them over and over again, closer and faster and sharper, until they become something much more than any of the pieces. They become something truly new and amazing to all who see it. And yet, even though our eyes have just been opened to something amazing, even "impossible!" the Blues' entire performance has been all about, "here's how we did this; normal people did this; come and do this with us." And that gives us a glimpse of how amazing we can be. That is the true human magic that the Blue Angels are all about.

With the 1969 season the team switched to the brawny F-4J Phantom, and in 1974, in order to reduce operational costs, to the elegant A-4F Skyhawk. The Skyhawk would become the team's longest-serving mount to date, lasting to the Blue's 40th anniversary in 1986.

But perhaps the Blues' most surprising and lasting star arrived in 1970 when the team's previous grab-bag of logistics support aircraft was replaced by a Lockheed KC-130F Hercules, soon to be named "Fat Albert." A Blues appearance is not complete without Albert's demonstration of a steep approach short-field assault landing in less than 2500 feet, complete with backing up on his reversible-pitch propellers, Old Glory streaming from the cockpit hatch. But the true highlight has been the short take-off capability provided by eight jet-assisted takeoff (JATO) bottles (actually solid-fueled rockets), attached to the rear fuselage. Fired simultaneously, the JATO bottles allow the big transport to take off within 1,500 feet, climb at a 45-degree angle, and reach an altitude of 1,000 feet in approximately 15 seconds. Sadly, the 2006 60th anniversary year is the last year that will see this memorable display. Fat Albert is the last of the American Hercules fleet to use the JATO bottles, and remaining stocks are running low. This makes the display too expensive, and since it no longer demonstrates a true operational

capability, it is being dropped from future seasons. But Fat Albert will continue to strut his stuff and deliver his message: "Yes, these are some hot little jets. But they can't do this without me, and I've got a couple of pretty slick moves of my own." There is Blue magic everywhere you look.

From 1946 to 1986 the Blues flew seven different aircraft. In their last twenty years, they have flown only one: the hunch-backed, aggressive F/A-18A Hornet. This aircraft brought the ability to perform a variety of new maneuvers, including low-speed, high-angle-of-attack passes. But as with any physical detail of the Blue Angels, the Hornet is a tool in the hands of the 125 members of the team, and its use will continue to evolve according to the excellence and creative magic of those members, melded into one single commitment to perfection.

Through the 2006 season, the Blue Angels have had 231 demonstration pilots and 31 flight leaders/commanding officers. By the end of the 2006 season, the Blue Angels have performed their demonstration for about 430 million fans, and the magic shows no sign of abating. Because it's not just about the flying, it's about *why the flying matters*. The flying matters because it's the result of 60 years of dedication to excellence by thousands of men and women to something they can't do by themselves; they can only do it by giving the best of what they've got to something bigger than they are, and believing that it will come back, amplified by the best of what their teammates have to offer. It's about trust, and belief, and faith, and giving oneself. And it works. The coordinated, committed, dedicated acts of 125 people just like anyone you've ever met combines to make magic. The flying matters because it shows us who and what we are, what we are capable of being, and how we get there. That is the Blue Angels' act of service. The same way that they will serve us by defending this nation when they return to the Fleet, they are serving us now. The Blue Angels show us all how to be magical.

The heat signatures from the six Boeing F/A-18 jets in the Diamond bends the shimmering sunlight reflected off the Gulf of Mexico just off the beach near NAS Pensacola. Three cheers to and SIXTY INCREDIBLE YEARS for the BLUE ANGELS and NAVAL AVIATION. TAILHOOKERS are without equal. Hip Hip Hooray! Hip Hip Hooray! Hip Hip Hooray!

US NAVY LEGACY FLIGHT

VFA-106 F/A-18F RHINO
LONE STAR F4U CORSAIR

First the long-nosed, dark blue tail-dragger sputters to life at the place of honor out near show center, spinning its big 13-foot propeller. As the aircraft taxis past the crowd, all are caught with the excitement of this beast stirring up the wind, and not a few wonder how the pilot can see around that huge nose.

– Essay by David C. Nilsen

Clockwise Top Left: Doug Rozendaal cranks the Corsair with LT Blaine "Rock" Tompkins and LT Matt "Sicko" Bernhard in the Rhino. From show center Rob Reider announces the Legacy Flight at the Monaco Air Show in Duluth, MN. with LCDR James "Plow" Lynch and LT Adam "Lil' Roo" Drayton. Doug readies for launch in front of Cirrus Design Headquarters. Previous/opposite pages: The Rhino and Corsair making turns en trail over Lake Superior.

Later, the sleek, haze gray jet slips from the other gray aircraft at the military hot ramp and whistles down the taxiway, awaiting a break in the airshow activity to launch. Like the blue machine before it, disappears over the horizon to orbit and await its turn in the day's schedule.

When they return, they do so from behind the crowd, and simply by flying together, are transformed into something inspiring. Even the casual airshow attendee knows that this is not something you see every day: an old propeller aircraft flying in formation with a big gray jet. And even the knowledgeable, who recognize the 50-year old Chance Vought F4U Corsair and the factory-fresh Boeing F/A-18F Super Hornet, know to drink it in, for this head-lifting, full-body experience is rare.

This is the US Navy Tailhook Legacy Flight.

The US Navy Tailhook Legacy Flight, in the bloodless prose favored by US government organizations, exists "to safely and proudly display the evolution of United States Naval airpower and to support the Navy and Marine Corps' recruiting and retention efforts. The services have determined that their recruiting efforts are enhanced by having fly-bys at air shows with vintage naval warbirds and F-18 aircraft."

Yeah, right. That probably works in some ring of the Pentagon, but the reason for the Legacy Flight is that it is a thing of beauty and inspiration, something that as the body absorbs the deep vibrations of that prop and two turbofans splitting the air, the spirit fills with a sense of the men and women who have sacrificed for a century to keep this country proud and free.

The Legacy Flight first flew at NAS Oceana in 1998, and is similar to the Air Force's Heritage Flight, which dates back to 1997. But to those who have been bit by the Naval Aviation bug, and "just say no" to 10,000 foot runways, the Tailhook Legacy Flight is the one-and-only Real Deal.

The speed of heat: Rock pulling vapes out of the humid summer air as the Rhino cranks past the crowd during the photo pass in full blower. Opposite: from the flight deck of the Coast Guard C-130 based in Sacramento, CA. Pilot LT Trocchio and Copilot Lt. Scott Murphy drive the Herc around the Split Rock Lighthouse so we could shoot out the open ramp..

The Legacy Flight brings us F4U and Goodyear-built FG Corsairs, Douglas AD Spads, F-8bs standing in for their blue and gull-gray FJ Fury sisters, F/A-18C Hornets, F/A-18E-F Super Hornets, and until last year, F-14 Tomcats, flying in formation in twos, threes, or fours.

Watching this magic, the similarities and contrasts come fast and furious. The prop aircraft are flying nose down, digging into the air for all they're worth, while the jets are throttled back, nose up, clawing to stay in the air on the wings of their older sisters.

But the prop planes are no mere antiques. These World War II and Korean War vets are the proud, snorting thoroughbreds of their day, and still represent the pinnacle of piston-powered performance, as any Reno fan knows. The Corsair was the first single-engine American fighter to break 400 mph in level flight (late models could hit 470), powered by Pratt & Whitney's legendary R-2800 Double Wasp engine, generating 1850 to ultimately 2500 horsepower in its final versions. This was America's first 18-cylinder radial engine, built in two rows of nine cylinders, and was the most powerful air-cooled engine in the world when introduced in 1939, and on par with the world's best liquid-cooled engines.

In order to harness this tremendous power, the Corsair was fitted with a huge 13 feet, 4 inch diameter propeller. The need to allow this large propeller arc to clear the ground while still having landing gear short and sturdy enough to survive carrier landings resulted in the Corsair's distinctive inverted gull-wing design, giving rise to its nickname, "bent-wing bird."

Although strange to think of today, the Navy originally barred the Corsair from carrier operations, deeming it unsuited to carrier landings in September 1942 carrier suitability trials. The Corsair landed too fast, had poor forward and downward visibility due to its big nose, and had excessive bounce. So the Corsair went into service as a land-based fighter, notably with the Marines in the Solomons Campaign, with such illustrious users as VMF-214, "The Black Sheep," and the Navy's VF-17 "Jolly Rogers."

While the easier-to-land F6F Hellcat embarked on its career as the Navy's top-scoring fighter (some 5100 kills), Chance Vought, Navy and Marine aviators worked to get the Corsair fit for carrier operations, and the Royal Navy just flew it off their carriers anyway, including against the German battleship *Tirpitz*. After several modifications, including improved aileron controls, a raised cockpit, and revised main gear oleos, the first US Navy carrier-based Corsair deployment had a detachment of F4U-2 night fighters from VF(N)-101 aboard USS *Enterprise* (CV 6) in January of 1944. Deployment of full squadrons of Corsairs on carriers began in December 1944 when two Marine squadrons deployed aboard USS *Essex* (CV 9). By the end of the war, and again in the Korean War, the Marines were regularly flying their bent-wing birds off of tiny jeep carriers, "these damned CVEs" as immortalized in the barroom song "Cuts and Guts":

> *Navy fliers fly off the big carriers*
> *Army fliers aren't seen o'er the sea*
> *But we're in the lousy Marine Corps*
> *So we get these damned CVEs!*

By war's end, the Corsairs had racked up 2140 kills at a loss of only 189 to aerial combat. Corsairs continued to serve through the Korean War, where they produced the Navy's only night fighter ace, LT Guy Bordelon, commemorated by the F4U-5 shown in the accompanying photos. In 1953 the 12,571st and last Corsair was delivered (to the French Navy, who used them in Indochina), making it the last propeller-driven fighter built in the US, as well as the longest-produced propeller fighter in US history.

Hanging onto the Corsair's wing is a relative baby, the F/A-18F Super Hornet, or "Rhino" as it is known around the boat. This aircraft is the follow-on, enlarged version of the F/A-18 Hornet, and successor to the mighty F-14 Tomcat, phased out of US service in September 2006. Unlike the Corsair, the Rhino is still unblooded in air-to-air combat (and even the great Tomcat only ever got 5 kills in US service—some sources credit Iranian Tomcats with as many as 193), and her legacy

This series of images are all pulled from the same photo flight over Lake Superior with the Split Rock Lighthouse as a backdrop on the North Shore. The Corsair is based down in Galveston. TX at the LONE STAR FLIGHT MUSEUM.

Opposite page shows both the Rhino getting wrung out by Rock and the inspiring Legacy Fly Bys. Above: Rock and Sicko taking a bow. Coast Guard C-130 crew (LtoR) AMT2 Ferry, LT Murphy, AMT1 Sanabia, LT Trocchio, AET1 Hanson, AMT3 McKenna and Ron Clark (USCG Aux) The Rhino ready to TRAP a 3-wire. Rock manning up.

will not be fully written for decades. But about these issues there is no argument: The "Super Bug" is newer than the Tomcat, requires fewer maintenance hours per flight hour, has newer electronics, and most important of all, is flown by the same squadrons that squired the Tomcat to her last dance: the Checkmates, Jolly Rogers, Pukin' Dogs, Red Rippers, Swordsmen, Blacklions, and Tomcatters. In hands like those, the Rhino will be a world-beater. Bet on it. That's what *legacy* means.

In contrast to the Corsair, which looks like it is wrapped around its single pilot, the twin-engined, supersonic, radar-equipped Rhino dwarfs its two aircrew. And when it separates from the venerable Corsair to demonstrate its own capabilities, it seems to do the aerodynamically impossible. Its digital control system allows it to point its nose well off its direction of flight, skidding and sliding through the skies, and maneuvering in the vertical like a rocket. But if you look closer, there is one similarity between the two birds that makes all the differences pale to insignificance: the little steel hook tucked beneath their tails.

In that one detail, the differences of the decades, of their technology, their respective wars and histories falls away. Both these birds, one the toughest beast of her day, the other the newest, "sports car" of now, are brought aboard the boat by day or night, in clear weather or pitching, rain-lashed fury, by catching a steel cable with that little steel hook. And if not, you go around until you do it right. It is this detail that has made people ask for decades, since James Michener first wrote it, "where do we get such men?" (And today, women too.)

That little hook, and all of the dedication that developed that system 80 years ago and has continued to execute and refine it under all conditions in the years since, is why there is no experience like the Legacy Flight. Why the odd assortment of aircraft tucked up next to each other: dainty Saber/Furies, snarling Corsairs, beefy Spads, sleek Hornets, massive Tomcats, are all sisters under the skin, and why we look up with pride at what we and our fellow Americans are capable of doing. And it keeps us coming back to see it one more time.

Thumbs up on a successful photo flight. Rock departs with a cliche' "Turn and Burn" Thanks to the Sacramento Herc crew and the US COAST GUARD for their support.

MUST SEE PILOTS

After publishing the first two editions of FRONT ROW CENTER, I realized that the FRC format prevents me from telling all the stories worthy of your attention. In an effort to make up for the somewhat narrow cross-section of the industry depicted in the stand-alone chapters, I present this new section to shine the spotlight on even more of the uniquely talented performers that certainly deserve chapters of their own someday. In a perfect world, I would have endless pages and an endless summer. Until then, I will do my best to keep bringing you FRONT ROW CENTER to the best and brightest of the airshow world. See you next time.

-Erik Hildebrandt

BILL STEIN   EDGE 540

SERGEI BORIAK   SU-31

DAVID BURDINE

MiG-17

ED HAMILL AIR FORCE RESERVE

JIM PEITZ

EXTRA 300L

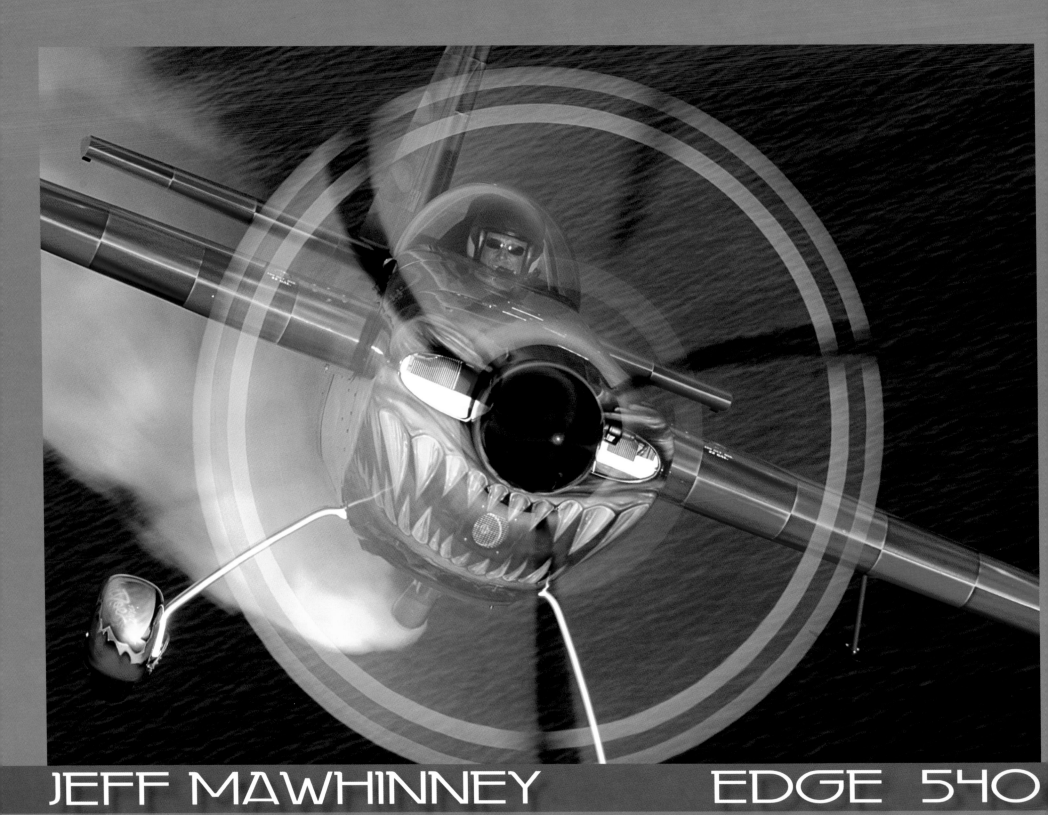

JEFF MAWHINNEY

EDGE 540

GREG POE   EDGE 540

HOT SHOTS 145

SKIP STEWART   PITTS S-2S

IRON EAGLE   CHRISTEN EAGLE

TIM WEBER

EXTRA 300

MiG-FURY   MiG-15/17 FJ-3 FURY

FLEET FLY BY   NAS OCEANA

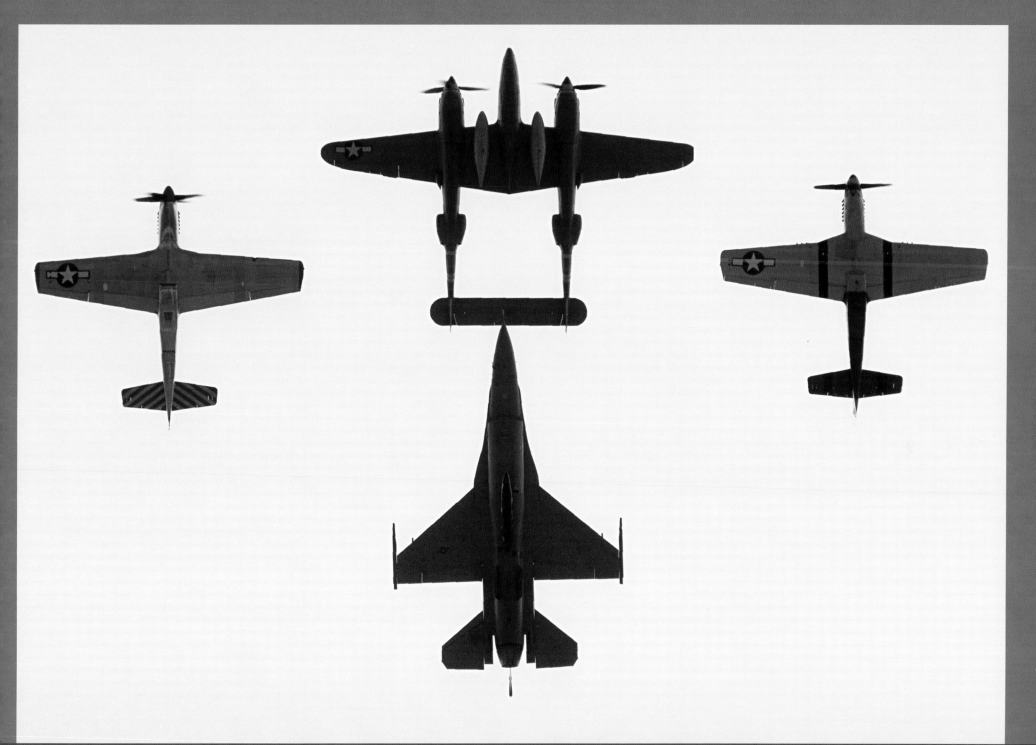

HERITAGE FLIGHT   OSHKOSH

GENE SOUCY   TERESA STOKES

FRC3 PHOTO MULE

O-2A

BOB ODEGAARD   SUPER CORSAIR

BONDO COSTELLO

ACC F-15

SNORT SNODGRASS   MUSTANG

MN AIR GUARD

F-16C

158 FRC3

BOB CARLTON   SILENT WINGS